P9-DTI-130

O MY JESUS

The Meaning of the Fátima Prayer

STEPHEN BULLIVANT
AND
LUKE ARREDONDO

Paulist Press
New York / Mahwah, NJ

Nihil obstat: Fr Julian Large, cong. Orat.
14th January 2017

Imprimatur: Most Rev Bernard Longley
Archbishop of Birmingham, UK
14th January 2017

The Scripture quotations contained herein are from the New Revised Standard Version: Catholic Edition, Copyright © 1989 and 1993, by the Division of Christian Education of the National Council of the Churches of Christ in the United States of America. Used by permission. All rights reserved.

Cover image by ChiccoDodiFC/Shutterstock.com
Cover design by Sharyn Banks
Book design by Lynn Else

Copyright © 2017 by Stephen Bullivant and Luke Arredondo

Library of Congress Cataloging-in-Publication Data
    Names: Bullivant, Stephen Sebastian, 1984– author.
    Title: O my Jesus : the meaning of the Fátima prayer / Stephen Bullivant and Luke Arredondo.
    Description: New York : Paulist Press, 2017. | Includes bibliographical references.
    Identifiers: LCCN 2016043795 (print) | LCCN 2017005785 (ebook) | ISBN 9780809153343 (pbk. : alk. paper) | ISBN 9781587686979 (ebook)
    Subjects: LCSH: Fatima, Our Lady of. | Mary, Blessed Virgin, Saint—Prayers and devotions. | Catholic Church—Prayers and devotions.
    Classification: LCC BT660.F3 B85 2017 (print) | LCC BT660.F3 (ebook) | DDC 242/.7—dc23
    LC record available at https://lccn.loc.gov/2016043795

ISBN 978-0-8091-5334-3 (paperback)
ISBN 978-1-58768-697-9 (e-book)

Published by Paulist Press
997 Macarthur Boulevard
Mahwah, New Jersey 07430
www.paulistpress.com

Printed and bound in the
United States of America

This book would not have been possible without Elena, my wife, whose sacrifices on my behalf never cease to amaze me, whose love never fails me, and whose joy and humility inspire me to be a better man every day. I thank God for my vocation to marry you and start a family, and for the children that we have been blessed to receive from the Lord, Faustina, Judith, Chiara, Therese, and Fulton. Te amo, Elena!

—Luke Arredondo

For David Bullivant, my father and fellow Santiago-pilgrim, who gamely accompanied me on my first (and so far only) visit to Fátima, and who is no doubt bemused by what it all has led to.

—Stephen Bullivant

Contents

Preface

*T*his is a little book about a tiny prayer regarding an unimaginably vast reality: the love and mercy of God. That tiny prayer, and the Portuguese town where it was first heard, played a small but significant role in my own journey toward discovering, embracing, and striving (however falteringly) to persevere within that reality.

This is not the place for that story—for it is a long one, and mostly boring—but it perhaps helps to explain the genesis of this book. Suffice it to say that, for some years now, I have wanted to write a book about the Fátima prayer. Even when *not* writing books about the Fátima prayer, in fact, I have done my best to find ways to include it.[1] Personal reasons aside, and as I hope the following pages prove, I am convinced that this brief prayer warrants sustained attention. It is, thanks to its popularity as a Rosary decade prayer, surely one of the Church's most-prayed prayers—perhaps even fourth, behind the Lord's Prayer, the Hail Mary, and the Glory Be. Furthermore, in the space of just twenty-nine words (including "amen"), only one of which is more than two syllables long, it broaches the great themes of the Christian message: sin, forgiveness, mercy, heaven, and hell.

In terms of structure, this book stands in a long tradition of works focusing on a single prayer: from Tertullian, St. Cyprian, and Origen's treatises on the Lord's Prayer in the second and third centuries, to Scott Hahn's *Understanding "Our Father"* in the twenty-first.[2] Like those, after a general introduction giving some background, it takes its subject line-by-line (or rather, clause-by-clause), devoting a chapter to each. Each chapter is intended to be part commentary (e.g., situating the clause within its wider context vis-à-vis the Fátima apparitions) and part theological and devotional reflection. With a prayer that is so often said quickly, and perhaps even automatically, either at the end of each Rosary decade or—as I do—just prior to receiving Holy Communion, it will hopefully prove rewarding to recite it prayerfully. It is certainly possible to sit and read this book straight through in a single sitting. But it might equally be worth spending a little time each day, reading a chapter at a time. For the true Fátima aficionados, the book could even be read over the five First Saturdays—if so, then it would be particularly good to combine chapters 3 and 4 into one.

Wanting to write a book of this sort, and having mentally mapped it in idle moments, I had simply been waiting for the impetus and time actually to write it.

The time never properly materialized—it never does—but the impetus of the Fátima Centenary in 2017 was obvious enough. What better excuse to persuade my friends at Paulist Press to risk publishing a book, much shorter than my usual ones, and on a subject in which I have no particular form? Happily, they were—as ever they are—very encouraging.

However, in July 2016, with an urgently looming deadline, only half a manuscript (and the rough half, at that), and several pages of roughly scribbled notes, I developed some health problems—mercifully, not permanent ones, but sufficiently non-fleeting enough to rule out finishing the book in anything like the required time. Rather than abandon the project, I asked my good friend, Luke Arredondo, if he might be willing, at such short notice, to coauthor it. Being the very epitome of Galatians 6:2: "Bear one another's burdens, and in this way you will fulfill the law of Christ," he kindly agreed.

The book you are holding is, in the fullest sense, a joint enterprise. (The one exception is this preface, which is Stephen's work alone.) My original chapters and notes have been thoroughly, and most beneficially, reworked by Luke. I, in turn, have felt at liberty to meddle with his drafts. Despite living at opposite sides of the Atlantic, and having met in person only once (at the excellent "Re-Engaging *Humanae Vitae*" conference, at Ave Maria University in Florida, earlier this year), we have a great deal in common, from each having several young daughters, to—critically here—sharing a fairly similar theological and neo-evangelistic outlook.[3]

I have wanted an excuse to collaborate with Luke for some time. I am accordingly proud to have my name sitting in such fine company on our front cover.

Stephen Bullivant
Bicester, UK
Feast of St. Clare of Montefalco, 2016

Introduction

A Historical Outline

*T*he following pages are a sustained theological reflection and meditation on the Fátima prayer, which is often prayed at the end of every decade of the Rosary. Before launching into the prayer itself, it will be helpful to situate ourselves within the world in which this prayer was delivered.

If we are to judge human affairs by their external appearances, it would seem that the consecration of a bishop in the Church would always be more important than a trio of young children taking their sheep out to pasture in the outskirts of a small village in Portugal. In fact, on May 13, 1917, Eugenio Pacelli's consecration as a bishop was certainly stamped with all the usual markers of importance.[1] But, as it so often happens in the life of the Church, the three simple shepherds, Lucia (age ten),

Jacinta (age seven), and Francisco (age nine), were perhaps engaged in an even more significant event. This date marked the first of six apparitions of a mysterious woman, robed in white and shining with a beautiful purity, who would later call herself Our Lady of the Rosary. She was from heaven, and had selected these three children to be the bearers of an important message.

St. Paul tells us that Jesus, "though he was in the form of God, / did not regard equality with God / as something to be exploited, / but emptied himself, / taking the form of a slave, / being born in human likeness. / And being found in human form" (Phil 2:6–7). Maybe, then, we should not be so surprised to learn that he would not send his Mother to visit the leaders of the world's most powerful nations, but instead, he would send her to seek out children. This was, after all, something Jesus indicated in the Gospels as well (see Matt 19:14). As St. John Paul II noted at the beatification of Jacinta and Francisco:

> In her motherly concern, the Blessed Virgin came here to Fátima to ask men and women "to stop offending God, Our Lord, who is already very offended." It is a mother's sorrow that compels her to speak; the destiny of her children is at stake. For this reason she asks the little shepherds: "Pray, pray much and make sacrifices for sinners; many souls go to hell because they have no one to pray and make sacrifices for them."[2]

Recall that this message was delivered in 1917; it was not recent. Mary's message was to prevent society from losing its way in an incredibly and increasingly secularized world. Taking into account the development of the world since 1917, we should intuitively grasp the way this message might need repeating even in our own day. Interestingly, though, this apparition of Mary in 1917 was not the first supernatural encounter these children had experienced. In fact, three years prior to Mary's visit, Lucia and a few other children who were tending their flocks near Fátima had seen "a figure like a statue made of snow which the rays of the sun had turned somewhat transparent."[3] Lucia and the other children endured quite a lot of humiliation for repeating this story, and nobody wanted to give it credit.

The next time Lucia had a spiritual encounter while shepherding, she and her young friends, Jacinta and Francisco, did manage to keep quiet about it. In fact, two years later, in 1916, the trio was visited three times by a figure who revealed himself as the "angel of Peace." This angelic visitor requested that the children pray these words: "My God, I believe, I adore, I hope, and I love You! I beg pardon of You for those who do not believe, do not adore, do not hope, and do not love You."[4]

On his second visit, he implored the young children to pray and hinted that the "hearts of Jesus and of Mary have merciful designs for you. Offer prayers and sacrifices constantly to the Most High." They were asked to begin to offer sacrifices "as an act of reparation for sinners by whom He is offended, and of supplication for the conversion of sinners." Finally, this mysterious angel visited a third time, and offered the children Holy Communion, which they were instructed to receive as an act of reparation and to console God, who had been "horribly insulted by ungrateful men."[5] Throughout their visits with this angel, the three shepherds managed not to repeat their stories or claims to their friends or family. The maturity, patience, and self-control needed to keep such a miraculous event secret perhaps showed that these children were ready to be the recipients of an even more august visitor just a year later.

THE FIRST APPARITION: MAY 13, 1917

While tending their sheep, a sudden and mysterious burst of light caused Lucia, Jacinta, and Francisco to run for cover. The light was so bright that they thought it could only have been a bolt of lightning. But they soon realized it was something altogether different. Instead of lightning, they saw before them a woman who was "more brilliant than the sun, and radiated a light more clear and intense than a crystal glass filled with sparkling water, when the rays of the burning sun shine through it."[6] She was dressed in a simple tunic, and held a Rosary in her hands. Eventually, this Woman spoke to them, saying, "Do not be afraid. I will do you no harm."[7] The Woman told the children that she was from heaven, and had a special request for them:

> I have come to ask you to come here for six
> months in succession, on the thirteenth day,
> at this same hour. Later on, I will tell you

who I am and what I want. Afterwards, I will
return here yet a seventh time.[8]

During their discussion with Mary at this first
apparition, the children were asked whether they
would be willing to suffer for sinners, and they were
also instructed to pray the Rosary "to obtain peace for
the world and the end of the war." Also in this dialogue,
Mary told Jacinta that she would go to heaven, as well
as her brother Francisco, but that he would "have to
pray many Rosaries."

THE SECOND APPARITION: JUNE 13, 1917

During this second apparition, Lucia notes that
Mary asked for those present to pray the Rosary *every
day*, and for the children to learn how to read. She also
announced that while Jacinta and Francisco would go
to heaven soon, Lucia would remain both as a witness
and to encourage people to be devoted to the Immaculate Heart of Mary.

THE THIRD APPARITION: JULY 13, 1917

This apparition was a major event, and one which
was initially ordered to be kept a secret by Mary herself. Crowds had begun to form on the thirteenth of
every month, but they were unable to hear the Woman's voice. Lucia asked the Woman to identify herself
and also for a miracle to be worked so that others

would believe in the apparitions. Mary responded that she would perform a miracle in October, and that she would reveal her identity at that time as well. She continued to stress the prayer of the Rosary for peace. Yet, the most fascinating part of this apparition is what is referred to as the first and second parts of the "secret of Fátima." During this appearance, Mary gave the children a vision of hell.[9] This vision is what Sister Lucia called the first part of the "secret."

After the terrifying vision of the punishment that sins were causing, Mary told Lucia that terrible consequences would result for the world if her instructions were not followed. This is the second part of the "secret." Mary warned that the war would go on, and an even greater war would break out during the pontificate of Pope Pius XI. These were her wishes:

> To prevent this, I shall come to ask for the consecration of Russia to my Immaculate Heart and the Communion of Reparation on the First Saturdays. If my requests are heeded, Russia will be converted, and there will be peace; if not, she will spread her errors throughout the world, causing wars and persecutions of the Church. The good will be martyred, the Holy Father will have much to suffer, and various nations will be annihilated. In the end, my Immaculate Heart will triumph. The Holy Father will consecrate Russia to me, and she will be converted, and a period of peace will be granted to the

world. In Portugal, the dogma of the Faith will always be preserved;…Do not tell this to anybody. Francisco, yes, you may tell him."[10]

This apparition is also important for us because it was on July 13, 1917, that the Fátima prayer was first given to the children. They were told to pray the words after each mystery of the Rosary.

THE LAST APPARITION: OCTOBER 13, 1917

For our purposes here, there is no need to examine the other apparitions. As silly as this may sound, they were *ordinary* apparitions in that Mary stressed the reality of sin, the importance of the Rosary, and the need for conversion. But in October, as promised, she delivered a miracle.

At the apparition on October 13, tens of thousands of pilgrims gathered. Lucia recounts how many humble souls would kneel in the presence of the three children, asking for cures, for conversion, and for many types of favors from Our Lady. Of course, plenty of skeptics were among those present, including a fair number of atheists.[11] It has been estimated that around seventy thousand people were there to see the sun "dance" in the sky, an incredibly powerful miracle. For Lucia, however, the vision also included the third part of the "secret." She notes,

> We saw an Angel with a flaming sword in his left hand; flashing, it gave out flames that

looked as though they would set the world on fire; but they died out in contact with the splendour that Our Lady radiated towards him from her right hand: pointing to the earth with his right hand, the Angel cried out in a loud voice: "Penance, Penance, Penance!" And we saw in an immense light that is God: "something similar to how people appear in a mirror when they pass in front of it" a Bishop dressed in White "we had the impression that it was the Holy Father." Other Bishops, Priests, men and women Religious going up a steep mountain, at the top of which there was a big Cross of rough-hewn trunks as of a cork-tree with the bark; before reaching there the Holy Father passed through a big city half in ruins and half trembling with halting step, afflicted with pain and sorrow, he prayed for the souls of the corpses he met on his way; having reached the top of the mountain, on his knees at the foot of the big Cross he was killed by a group of soldiers who fired bullets and arrows at him, and in the same way there died one after another the other Bishops, Priests, men and women Religious, and various lay people of different ranks and positions. Beneath the two arms of the Cross there were two Angels each with a crystal aspersorium in his hand, in which they gathered up the blood of the

Martyrs and with it sprinkled the souls that were making their way to God."[12]

When John Paul II was nearly assassinated on May 13, 1981, he immediately sensed a connection to Fátima. Even while in the hospital, he asked to be brought the text of the third part. Later on, he would famously say that while his assassin did "shoot to kill," it was "as if someone was guiding and deflecting that bullet."[13] Yet, as the text indicates, if the apparition were to have been an exact prediction of the future, it couldn't have pointed to John Paul II, could it? This is precisely the question that the Congregation for the Doctrine of the Faith addressed in "The Message of Fatima." The prudence of Lucia not to reveal the entirety of the vision when it was first received comports well with the Church's attitude toward private revelation. As Cardinal Ratzinger noted, the prophetic vision of Fátima, like the text of Sacred Scripture, "[does] not describe photographically the details of future events."[14]

The enduring value, then, of Fátima, or any private revelation, is its relevance in increasing the faith of the Church. This means that the ultimate value of the apparitions was not in their ability to predict history, however accurately they may have done so. Instead, they point toward a more fundamental concern: "Our Lady's call to conversion and penance," which "remains timely and urgent today."[15] In the wider view, the Church tells us that even those private revelations approved by the Church should be understood as a "help which is offered, but which one is not obliged to use."[16]

With this background and an appreciation of the scope of the Fátima apparitions, and Our Lady's concern for sin, the danger of hell, and the prospect of conversion, let us now turn to the words of the prayer she first taught to the three young shepherds. May it bear fruit in our own souls just as it did in theirs, and as it has in the century since the Church received it.

1
O my Jesus

"*O* my Jesus" is not a mode of address that comes naturally to us. For how could it? Who dares to speak to the "Lord of glory" (1 Cor 2:8) in so familiar, so intimate a fashion? Who would presume to be on first-name terms with the "saviour of the universe"?[1]

In the Gospels, not a single one of our Lord's closest followers addresses him directly by name. Most often, they call him *Kyrios*, which—like *Señor* in Spanish or *Herr* in German—can mean "sir" or "Lord." This is a term that makes unmistakably clear a certain amount of deference and respect. Peter, for example, uses it when asking theological questions: "Lord, are you telling this parable for us or for everyone?" (Luke 12:41). He uses it when in mortal panic: "Lord, save me!" (Matt 14:30). He uses it when pledging his enduring fidelity: "Lord, you know everything; you know that I love you" (John 21:17), and even when actually arguing with Jesus:

"God forbid it, Lord!" (Matt 16:22), he is still careful to signal his deference and respect with this title.

Other such titles, used by the disciples and others, have a similar role. Judas addresses Jesus with *rabbi*, the Hebrew word meaning "teacher," several times (e.g., Mark 14:45; Matt 26:25, 49), but so too, on various occasions, do Nathanael, Nicodemus, Peter, and "the disciples" as a whole. Mary Magdalene calls the risen Christ *rabbouni*, the Aramaic version of *rabbi* (John 20:16).

Jesus *is* spoken to by name several times, however. Most of these occasions fall into two main types: demons, revealing their supernatural insight to *who* precisely he is and why he has come (e.g., Mark 1:24); and strangers, humbly begging Jesus to have mercy on them. Luke has his lepers implore, "Jesus, Master, have mercy on us!" (17:13; see also 18:38; Mark 10:47–48). Note that in each of these cases, even though Jesus is indeed named, some other, more formal mode of address is swiftly added. Even in the situation of total despair, for those who were already outcast by their situations, a personal and intimate form of address is too risky.

But there is nothing like that in the Fátima Prayer: just "O my Jesus." Peter and the disciples, Mary Magdalene, the desperately ill hoping for a personal cure, even the demons…not one is so bold as to speak so informally with "my Lord and my God" (John 20:28). So how then can we?

At the end of Luke's Gospel, God himself, scourged and humiliated, hangs dying on two rough planks of wood. Perversely, in this degradation he is surrounded by titles and terms of respect. His claims to be the

Savior, indeed "the Messiah of God, his chosen one" (23:35), are turned against him in mockery. Above his head, a sign sarcastically proclaims him "the King of the Jews" (Luke 23:38).

It is on this occasion only that we find that the Messiah is addressed by his first name: "Jesus, remember me when you come into your kingdom" (Luke 23:42).

These words, of course, come from the repentant thief. They are spoken out of true humility. He acknowledges his own guilt and regards himself as justly condemned. He is beyond hope of reprieve. Offered the opportunity to ask the Christ for anything at all, he asks not for rescue or redemption, but merely to be remembered.

And yet the one that miserable thief speaks to, the one whom he believes will soon come into his kingdom, is likewise a condemned criminal. Jesus is indeed "the Messiah of God, his chosen one." He is "the King of the Jews." But he is these things precisely because he can be addressed as a social equal by an abject, and justly condemned, sinner. The two men—one executed; the other murdered—hang side-by-side as social equals. From the most unexpected person, a condemned thief, Jesus is addressed by name. In so doing, the thief, in the inimitable words of Venerable Fulton Sheen, "died a thief, for he stole Paradise."[2]

This is, of course, precisely the point of the incarnation: God himself comes to hang beside us, as a "man among men";[3] the only one who can offer us the mercy we need, alongside us as one of whom we might actually dare to ask for mercy. And this is, more or less, the overriding message of Fátima: that while we—all of us—are in dire need of mercy, we're on first-name terms with him on whom we have to call. Like the father of the prodigal son, even our sinfulness doesn't keep Jesus from wanting to embrace us, restore our dignity, and offer us a feast in celebration of our return.

We might better grasp the distinctiveness, the deceptive simplicity, of the Fátima Prayer when we compare it to an even more famous prayer. Like the Fátima Prayer, the ancient Jesus Prayer acknowledges the sinfulness of the person praying, and implores the divine mercy.[4] Also like the Fátima Prayer, it is short, suitable for mantra-like repetition, and easily prayed from the heart. But note the differences: "*Lord Jesus Christ, Son of God*, have mercy on me, a sinner." These titles are of course all true and important. Jesus is indeed our Lord, the Christ, the coequal Son of God the Father: if he were not, then sinners would seek for mercy in vain. But they are rather different from the directly personal mode of speech of the thief whom Jesus promised: "Truly I tell you, today you will be with me in Paradise" (Luke 23:43).

Fátima goes further still. The crucified thief—condemned by the law; pardoned, indeed exalted, by grace—feels able, unselfconsciously, to call him just Jesus. Yet, even he does not presume to call him *my* Jesus. For once again, who could? I can think of only two types of people—and so, with a moment's thought, can you.

"The Lord of glory," God incarnate, has a mom and stepdad. And to answer the question posed in a popular Christmas song, Mary certainly *did know*. She knew full well—indeed, she had an archangel's word for it—that her unborn child, conceived by the Holy Spirit, was the "Son of the Most High" (Luke 1:26–38).

Yet for all that, we cannot but suppose that, to Mary of Nazareth, he was and will always be "my Jesus." The baby whom she had birthed, even heralded by a soundtrack from the heavenly host (Luke 2:13–14). The infant whose diapers and tantrums she endured, even with the full knowledge he was heir apparent of the throne of David (1:32). The young man whom she saw tortured to death before her eyes (John 19:25), even remembering the assurances that "of his kingdom there will be no end" (Luke 1:33). Through all this, from the Annunciation until the end of time, how could she possibly think of him as anything other than "my Jesus"? This is precisely why St. John Paul II, in his apostolic letter on the Rosary in 2002, encouraged all the faithful not merely to pray the Rosary, but to do so "through the eyes" of Mary.[5] This method of prayer invites us deep into the personal communion with our Lord that Mary quite appropriately enjoyed as his mother.

The opening words of the Fátima Prayer, then, are just what one might expect from a prayer of a mother about her son. "O my Jesus," or rather its Aramaic equivalent, is perhaps a phrase she uttered many times—in joy, in exasperation (our Lord was, of course, once a three-year-old boy), in sorrow; and always, naturally, with love.

Remember, too, those to whom this prayer was first entrusted: three young children, of elementary school age—Jacinta, age seven; her brother, Francisco, age nine; and their cousin Lucia, age ten. These bright young shepherds, though certainly devout, were not *quite* the super-pious caricatures of popular devotion. True, they would pray the Rosary while out on the hills—well, sort of. Lucia, herself, charmingly tells us how the children used to cut corners while out tending sheep:

> We had been told to say the Rosary after our lunch, but as the whole day seemed too short for our play, we worked out a fine way of getting through it quickly. We simply passed the beads through our fingers, saying nothing but "Hail Mary, Hail Mary, Hail Mary…." At the end of each mystery, we paused awhile, then simply said "Our Father" and so, in the twinkling of an eye, as they say, we had our Rosary finished![6]

Nevertheless, for all their understandably childish "eagerness to get to our play,"[7] their simple, instinctive love for Jesus was never in doubt.

Just like the children who flocked to Jesus in the Gospels, our Portuguese shepherds felt perfectly at liberty to approach him similarly in prayer. Bear in mind, too, that children tend to be more honest than adults about their feelings of ownership and possession. (As my eldest daughter once said to me, "No, Daddy! Mummy is *not* your wifey. She is *my* wifey now!") "My Jesus" is a perfectly natural and laudable way for a child to think of him. Likewise, "O my Jesus" is a suitably direct, and one might even say blunt, way for them to start a prayer.

The humility of this prayer, the method by which it was given to the world, through the mediation of peasants in a remote village in Portugal, and its simple and direct language, are all stunning aspects of the prayer that ought not be overlooked. We have before us what purports to be, at least, a very special set of words. A prayer revealed by heaven, itself, for poor sinners to entreat God's mercy—and one whose messenger, indeed perhaps its author, is the Mother of God, herself. Furthermore, it is one that could be entrusted to the memories of three children, for *them* to go and teach it to the universal Church—indeed, to the whole world. Those opening words, "O my Jesus," ring true on all three counts. These are words deep enough to echo the humble thief's cry to a God who humbled himself enough to hear it:

> Christ Jesus,
> who, though he was in the form of God,
>> did not regard equality with God
>> as something to be exploited,
> but emptied himself,

taking the form of a slave,
being born in human likeness.
And being found in human form,
he humbled himself
and became obedient to the point of
death—
even death on a cross.

(Phil 2:5–8)

But they are equally tender, loving, and unselfconscious enough to be the words of both a mother concerning her son—a "personal relationship with Jesus" if ever there was one—and of three poor children addressing their dear Lord.

Scripture and Tradition put each of these before us as models for our own prayer lives. According to the fifth-century pope, St. Leo the Great, for instance, "The believing robber's faith was a type of those who are to be saved."[8] In the words of St. John Paul II, "For the People of God, Mary represents the model of every expression of their prayer life. In particular, she teaches Christians how to turn to God to ask for his help and support in the various circumstances of life."[9] Finally, Christ himself tells us that it is children we must emulate: "Truly I tell you, unless you change and become like children, you will never enter the kingdom of heaven. Whoever becomes humble like this child is the greatest in the kingdom of heaven" (Matt 18:3–4). And it was, let us not forget, a far younger child than Jacinta, Francisco, and Lucia who was the first to recognize him, jumping for joy as he did so (Luke 1:44). In uttering the Fátima

Prayer, then, we are praying alongside, and in unison with, each of these exemplars in the Communion of Saints.

REFLECTION QUESTIONS

1. When praying "O my Jesus," do I really mean it? That is, do I seek a meaningful and personal relationship with Jesus? Do I invite him into my life in an integral way, or do I keep Jesus at arm's length, careful not to let him get too close to me?

2. What can I learn from the children in my life about the simplicity that I ought to have in my relationship with Jesus? How can I both set an example for young people and learn from them at the same time?

3. How can I pray just the Fátima Prayer, in my mind and out loud, throughout the day, as a way of trying to "pray always," as we're told by St. Paul?

4. When I pray the Rosary, do I fly through the words of the Fátima Prayer without considering their deep significance? How can I better appreciate the power of these simple words?

2

Forgive us our sins

*T*he opening line of the Fátima Prayer immediately places the pray-er on a personal, intimate footing with "my Jesus." But then, just as immediately, this individual and private notion of "my Jesus" is expanded to become a much more universal prayer. One might say that these words help us to unite the vertical dimension of prayer, which concerns our relationship to the Lord of creation, with the horizontal, which is our connection to one another.

For while praying the Fátima Prayer is, indeed, to speak as a mother to her son, as a dying felon to his fellow convict, or as peasant children to their Lord, it is, critically, also to pray *for* others: "Forgive *us our* sins." And who, precisely, is "us"? It is, as the prayer itself soon makes clear, "all souls." That is to say, absolutely everybody.

This is quite a shift in the space of a few words: from a lone individual to the whole of humanity. But of course, that is often enough how salvation history works. As Paul famously puts it:

> Therefore just as one man's trespass led to condemnation for all, so one man's act of righteousness leads to justification and life for all. For just as by the one man's disobedience the many were made sinners, so by the one man's obedience the many will be made righteous. (Rom 5:18–19)

The Christian stands right in the middle of this drama, a blood relative of both Adam and Christ; justly condemned as the former's coconspirator, but promised glory as the latter's friend (John 15:14–15), sibling (Mark 3:35; Eph 1:5), and coheir (Rom 8:17); an individual caught up in the grand adventure of humanity as a whole, and with a personal role to play. In the words of the Elder Zosima, from Dostoevsky's *The Brothers Karamazov*, "Each is responsible before all, and for everything."[1]

Our prayer, like the message of Fátima as a whole, is one of hope. In order to understand this hope properly, we must first speak of other things. As Pope Francis has noted, it is important for Christians to talk about "things…in a context."[2] Our subject here is a case in point.

"*Forgive* us our *sins*." We can make no sense of the first word here, unless understood in the context of the last. In fact, the same goes for all the great headlines of the Christian good news: repentance, mercy, reconciliation, redemption, and salvation. None of them makes an iota of sense without sin. And not just a little bit of sin, but a vast, fetid pile of it, hidden deep within…well, *us* and even…*me*. Possibly one of the most unfashionable things to speak of in the modern era, but one that bears repeating and something of which we all need to be reminded, is the reality of sin, not just as an abstract concept like the Force (or, God help us, midi-chlorians), but as a brute fact of our fallen human nature that stands in need of redemption. The reality of sin, then, is a personal affair, just as much as it is a universal problem. It unites again, the vertical and horizontal.

Perhaps the magnitude of this problem is better grasped by reflecting on the sheer extravagance of the means by which God chose to rectify it. The power and ingenuity of the triune God is proclaimed throughout an observable universe—created by fiat, let's not forget—of some ninety-three billion light years across. And yet, the depth of human disobedience could, it would seem, only be fixed through a scheme that Scripture itself admits looks like "foolishness" (1 Cor 1:18).

The real God had to become a real man, really die—in fact, he was murdered[3]—and really rise again. (Incidentally, each one of those "reals" reflects a necessary point of doctrine, hard-won in the Church's first few centuries.) If that was actually the easiest solution, how intractable must have been the problem? How enormous must human sinfulness be, if the Almighty has, literally, to take matters into his own hands (and feet)?

This point may be usefully illustrated with examples taken from both the teaching and witness of our present Holy Father. Francis is himself, in continuity with a string of his predecessors, a devotee of Fátima. Just six months after becoming Pope, he consecrated the whole world to Our Lady of Fátima, before a crowd of some 150,000 pilgrims in St. Peter's Square.[4] Presumably, too, it did not escape his notice that the Year of Mercy overlaps with the beginnings of the centenary of the apparitions at Fátima.[5]

Take, for example, from an interview given in the first year of his pontificate, Francis's answer to the question "Who is Jorge Mario Bergoglio?":

> I am a sinner. This is the most accurate definition. It is not a figure of speech....I am a sinner....Here, this is me, a sinner on whom the Lord has turned his gaze. And this is what I said when they asked me if I would accept my election as pontiff..."I am a sinner, but I trust in the infinite mercy and patience of our Lord Jesus Christ, and I accept in a spirit of penance."[6]

While we have by now, perhaps, become accustomed to the Holy Father's self-effacing statements, it is worth noting that Francis's humility here is not at all like Uriah Heep's: a purely formal show of being "ever so 'umble."[7] Instead, it expresses a central conviction of the Christian faith.

For the Christian, the searing guilt one feels for one's sins is, or ought to be, underwritten with hope in the One who is "rich in mercy" (Eph 2:4). With great sorrow at having sinned comes the greater appreciation of him who is able, and willing, to forgive us. Thus the famous words of Timothy: "The saying is sure and worthy of full acceptance, that Christ Jesus came into the world to save sinners—of whom I am the foremost" (1 Tim 1:15). Or as Paul writes, "God proves his love for us in that while we still were sinners Christ died for us" (Rom 5:8) and "where sin increased, grace abounded all the more" (5:20). From Paul and Augustine, right down to Dorothy Day and Mother Teresa, it is always the saints who are most painfully aware of how sinful they are, of how desperately they need God's mercy. This sounds counterintuitive, but it is always those closest to perfection who realize how far they really are from reaching their goal. We shall have much more to say on this theme in chapter 5.

Here, though, we may emphasize again that the reality, ubiquity, and gravity of sin are at the very heart of the Christian message. Simply put, if we do not acknowledge our sins, then we fail to appreciate the One whose forgiveness is even stronger than sin—who can, to quote again from *The Brothers Karamazov*, "forgive everything, forgive all *and for all*, because he himself gave his innocent blood for all and for everything."[8] Without sin, we would have no debt in need of redemption, no estrangement in need of reconciliation, no just sentence against which to receive, with awesome thankfulness and joy, mercy.

If "sin" is a concept that has fallen out of fashion, the word seems not to have reached Casa Santa

Marta. Pope Francis uses it often, and not only when he speaks candidly of his own "faults and...sins."[9] As is well-known, he talks about forgiveness and mercy a great deal. But—and this fact often gets lost in the reporting—he rarely ever shuts up about sin either. Early on in his pontificate, it became a steady and consistent feature of his daily homilies to talk frankly of the reality of sin and of our need for forgiveness. However, as the Year of Mercy was under preparation, he noted that in order to fully understand mercy, the Church needs to proclaim also a "theology of sin." The result is his book-length interview, *The Name of God is Mercy*, where he elaborates on the relationship between mercy and sin: "To follow the way of the Lord, the Church is called on to dispense its mercy over all those *who recognize themselves as sinners*, who assume responsibility for *the evil they have committed*, and who *feel in need of forgiveness*" (my emphases).[10]

Significantly, the Holy Father is also on record as criticizing the confessor who is "too lax," who "washes his hands by simply saying, 'This is not a sin.'"[11] Thus Francis's "field hospital"—to use one of his favored images of the Church[12]—is there to *heal* wounds, not deny that they exist. This is, of course, a mission it shares with its Senior Consultant: "Those who are well have no need of a physician, but those who are sick; I have come to call not the righteous but sinners" (Mark 2:17).

Francis has also been known to quote Pope Pius XII's 1946 warning to a group of American catechists that "perhaps the greatest sin in the world today is that men have begun to lose the sense of sin."[13] If even traditionally sin-obsessed Catholics have, in recent decades, lost a keen sense of sin (as freefalling—or rather, by now, long since freefall*en*—statistics for Confession suggest), what hope is there for the rest of the world? This is a worry that impacts upon the prospects of the New Evangelization as a whole. But there are signs of hope. Pope Francis, who may well be more known for his comments about not judging others, has made it clear that he still considers himself less than perfect. Thus, he has often made the headlines for going to confession out in the open, just like a normal human being, aware of the fact that he is a sinner. In an American context, Timothy Cardinal Dolan, of New York, has also stated that when he goes to confession, he often stands in line just like everybody else, and that he uses the screen![14] Still, much remains to be done to encourage Catholics to go to confession in larger numbers, and one important part of that is to realize we have, in fact, sinned.

More to the point, in order to receive the good news *as* good news, it is surely essential that we recognize *ourselves* in Paul's assertion that "all have sinned and fall short of the glory of God" (Rom 3:23). For if we are not sinners—and if we are not, at least sometimes and however inadequately, heartrendingly sorrowed by that very fact—then what exactly do we imagine that Jesus Christ has come to save us from?

It is surely no coincidence that sin-and-forgiveness should be so prominent in the devotions entrusted to the little shepherd-seers of Fátima. The same is true of the message of Divine Mercy entrusted to St. Faustina Kowalska a little over a decade later. Both arose at a time when humanity was showing itself, on an unprecedentedly global scale, to be in desperate need of salvage.

Certainly, it was a message that the little seers themselves, as true "teachers and witnesses,"[15] took greatly to heart. According to Lucia, this was most clearly the case with the youngest of the three. Blessed Jacinta, all of seven, had had Our Lady's assurances that she would herself go to heaven. Far from breeding complacency, this impressed upon her that others' happy fates were not so guaranteed. Offering prayers and sacrifices on behalf of the sins of other people became her abiding concern. One example must stand here for the many that Lucia relates:

> There was a woman in our neighborhood who insulted us every time we met her. We came upon her once, as she was leaving a tavern, somewhat the worse for drink. Not satisfied with mere insults, she went still further. When she had finished, Jacinta said to me: "We have to plead with Our Lady and offer sacrifices for the conversion of this woman. She says so many sinful things that if she doesn't go to confession, she'll go to hell."
>
> A few days later, we were running past this woman's door when suddenly Jacinta stopped dead, and turning round, she asked:

"Listen! Is it tomorrow that we're going to see the Lady?"

"Yes, it is."

"Then let's not play anymore. We can make this sacrifice for the conversion of sinners."[16]

There are, perhaps, aspects of some of Lucia's vignettes that might trouble contemporary readers—in fact, there are enough aspects that would have troubled the children's parents and priests at the time too (none of whom, I suspect, would have condoned sacrificing their lunches to their sheep, or "offering up" the sting of deliberately grasped nettles[17]). But even if so, their overall spirit is one to which we certainly can, and should, still relate. This consciously taking upon ourselves, in prayer and penance, responsibility not just for our own failings, but those of others too, is something we have perhaps lost.

Of course, this responsibility is not lost when we pray the Fátima Prayer: "Forgive us our sins." There is another famous prayer Catholics know very well that repeats a similar line, and surely this cannot be a mere coincidence. In the Our Father, we ask God to "forgive us our trespasses" just as we do in the Fátima Prayer. St. Thomas Aquinas, though he is famous for many other things, is well-known for stating that the Our Father is the "most perfect" of prayers.[18] It's hard not to argue with that kind of lofty praise for this prayer when, after all, it was the Lord himself who revealed it. Yet, while Aquinas is surely correct, might we say that here in the Fátima Prayer, we have almost a summary of the Our Father? It seems that in some ways the children of Fátima were taught a simpler version, one more suitable for the youthful innocence of the souls like the children to whom it was revealed, but at the same time more direct, for a world more in need of God's salvation. In any event, praying in this fashion, we follow the example of little Jacinta, in heaven as she was on earth. As she once told Lucia,

> [When I am in Heaven] I'm going to love Jesus very much, and the Immaculate Heart of Mary, too. I'm going to pray a lot for you, for sinners, for the Holy Father, for my parents and my brothers and sisters, and for all the people who have asked me to pray for them.[19]

The notion of asking Jesus to "forgive *us our* sins" clearly builds a bridge of solidarity between our individual spiritual lives and that of the Body of Christ. But at the same time, it reminds us of the gravity and reality of sin, which we will discuss more in the next chapter. It is fitting, then, to recall that St. John Paul II, echoing Dostoevsky's Father Zosima, once wrote in another context, "We are all really responsible for all."[20]

REFLECTION QUESTIONS

1. What is it about the contemporary world that makes it so easy to lose the sense of sin, as Pope Pius XII said to the American catechists? Have

things gotten better or worse on that front since 1946, when he made that claim?

2. In my own spiritual life, am I truly aware of my sins? Do I truly recognize that Jesus wants to heal us, and that it means we must admit we are in need of healing?

3. This part of the prayer has us say "forgive us our sins." Do we take up the model of the children of Fátima and pray not only for our own sins, but also for those of other people? Or do we take the more common route of pointing out the sins of others while ignoring our own failings?

4. What are some ways to be honest in our spiritual life without becoming too obsessive or scrupulous about our sinfulness? How can the Fátima Prayer help us in this regard?

3

Save us from the fires of hell

We saw in the last chapter how forgiveness and mercy—core concepts in the Christian vocabulary —make no sense at all unless against the backdrop of sin. Something similar is true of another core concept: salvation. Jesus has indeed come to save the world (see John 3:17). But just as this salvation has an ultimate destination—a "place" that we will discuss in the next chapter—there is also an ultimate destination *from* which he has come to save us. It is this "somewhere" to which the Fátima Prayer now turns our attention.

Hell isn't as popular as it used to be. Surveys consistently show that while lots of people still believe in heaven (including—curiously enough—a good number of atheists[1]), rather fewer believe in hell. And that trend is as true of Catholics as it is of everybody else. Indeed, there are Catholic theologians who have written whole books about heaven and salvation, while barely mentioning hell at all.[2]

In such a climate, the message of Fátima does not necessarily sit easily. But then, neither—and this really ought to give us pause—does the message of Jesus of Nazareth.

Jesus talks about hell, *gehenna* in New Testament Greek, an awful lot. True enough, it is not a subject he ever dwells on in detail: there is no suite of parables that intimate various aspects of hell, as there are for its opposite, the kingdom (see Mark 4; Matt 13). But Jesus refers to it in all main strands of the gospel tradition.[3] And what he does say, though brief, is often graphically to the point. *"Fires of hell,"* the specific phrase used at Fátima, is a thoroughly Jesuanic image (Mark 9:43; Matt 13:42, 50; 25:41).

This recognition explains the urgency we find in the Gospels. From his emergence from the wilderness ("repent, and believe in the good news," Mark 1:15) to his postresurrection farewell tour ("repentance and forgiveness of sins is to be proclaimed...to all nations," Luke 24:47), Jesus is, most literally, a Godman on a mission.[4] We see the same sense of zeal, of course, in many of the great saints (not excluding, we might add, Jacinta Marto).

In fact, there was an obscure priest from France who showed a particular care for saving people from these fires, the Curé of Ars. When St. John Vianney received his parish assignment, Ars was a virtually unknown town, and the prospects for becoming a saint might have seemed unlikely. His bishop even told him, "There is not much love of God in that parish, you will put some there."[5] One might rightly say that the principal method John Vianney used to bring a love of God to his parishioners was to encourage them to frequent the sacrament of confession. St. John Paul II notes that Vianney spent ten hours a day, and occasionally even fifteen hours, in the confessional, trying to plead with the souls that came to him there, calling those to perfection who were seeking it, but weeping for some sinners who didn't seem to understand the gravity of their own sins. It will help to recall that Vianney was a priest in France at a time after the revolution had all but destroyed the Church. Certainly, the idea of thousands of souls flocking to him from all over Europe to confess their sins would have sounded ludicrous when he began his ministry as a priest. But over time, this is precisely what happened. Against all odds, Vianney maintained an awareness of what was at stake and was able to make a profound impact on the world. This serious trust in confession as the means to avoid sin and avoid hell is something we ought to remember in a world that faces very serious and loud objections to the notion of hell. In fact, in the 2009 Year of the Priest, Pope Benedict XVI noted,

> At the time of the Curé of Ars, confession was
> no more easy or frequent than in our own day,

since the upheaval caused by the revolution had long inhibited the practice of religion. Yet he sought in every way, by his preaching and his powers of persuasion, to help his parishioners to rediscover the meaning and beauty of the sacrament of Penance, presenting it as an inherent demand of the Eucharistic presence. He thus created a *"virtuous" circle*.[6]

While it is common today to speak, rightly so, of the Eucharist as the "source and summit" of the faith (*Lumen Gentium* 11), it is also important to keep reconciliation in focus. This is something of which the Fátima Prayer reminds us. It takes some getting used to for some of us in the modern world to talk openly about the concept of hell, let alone the possibility that *we* might end up there. But that is one of the brilliant things about this pithy prayer: it speaks to what is critical for us to remember, and does so with childlike honesty and simplicity.

As noted above, Jesus uses "fire" as a description of what precisely he has come to call sinners away *from*. It is important to point out that Jesus' images are not always to be understood in a literal way. For instance, the kingdom of God probably isn't, in all its details, exactly like a housewife baking an absurdly large amount of bread (Matt 13:33).[7] The primary focus of judgement day will not be on actual farm animals (Matt 25:31–33). And Jesus did not really sprout grapes from his body (John 15:1). But we ignore the stark, deliberately scary images with which Jesus chooses to illustrate hell at our, and others', peril. There might not be a genuine "immortal underground worm"[8] (see Mark 9:48; Isa 66:24) accompanying the unhappy souls. But if it is indeed a metaphor, then it scarcely bodes well concerning what *does* await them.

The same "beautiful Lady"[9] who appeared at Fátima once told the steward of the wedding at Cana in Galilee, "Do whatever he tells you" (John 2:5). Sound advice! And it would certainly include a prudent concern for others and oneself not to end up in a state of "definitive self-exclusion from communion with God and blessed" (*Catechism of the Catholic Church* [CCC] 1033).

It is in light of this that one of the more controversial aspects of the Fátima apparitions may be properly appreciated. Against the backdrop of Jesus' own words, we can see how "the message of Fátima...with its urgent call to conversion and penance, draws us to the heart of the gospel."[10]

The so-called first secret (or first part of the "secret") of Fátima, originally revealed on July 13, 1917, consists of a chilling vision of hell: "She opened her hands.... The rays of light seemed to penetrate the earth, and we saw as it were a sea of fire."[11] The full description, even though "the vision lasted but an instant,"[12] is certainly not for the fainthearted. While we need not dwell on the graphic details here,[13] it is important to make two points. The first is simply to reiterate, yet again, that Jesus himself, and the rest of the New Testament with him (e.g., 2 Thess 2:8–9; Rev 14:9–11; 20:10, 14–15), can also be terrifyingly graphic; the second is to say that the *specific* images presented in the Fátima revelations need not, as then-Cardinal Ratzinger put it in 2000, be interpreted as exact representations of the realities they seek to convey: "Such visions…are never simple 'photographs' of the other world."[14] Nevertheless, if one does regard them as authentic—and such private revelations, even ones approved by the Church, are not binding on the faithful—one must admit that whatever ultimate realities they *symbolize*, they are probably ones of which we should be exceedingly mindful.

The Fátima Prayer was itself revealed soon after the vision of hell, right at the close of the July 1917 apparition. Although Our Lady herself suggested that "when you pray the Rosary, say [it] after each decade," the children would themselves also use it as a standalone prayer. Francisco uttered it prior to making his confession before his first—and tragically last—holy communion, as he lay dying during the Spanish influenza epidemic in April 1919.[15] Lucia recollects that Jacinta, who would die of the same illness early the following year, would recite it "often" when struck by fears regarding others' eternal fate:

> Shuddering, she knelt down with her hands joined, and recited the prayer that Our Lady had taught us…Jacinta remained on her knees like this for long periods of time, saying the same prayer over and over again.[16]

Note here the extent to which, from its very origins, the Fátima Prayer is a prayer *for others*. In fact, we are reminded of the biblical injunction to "pray for one another, so that you may be healed" (James 5:16), or indeed that "supplications, prayers, intercessions, and thanksgivings be made for everyone" (1 Tim 2:1).

In the previous chapter, we noted the communal, social, or horizontal aspect of the Fátima Prayer. While built upon an intimate, personal relationship with "my Jesus," the root concern of the prayer is not with the *individual* at all. Its form, as we have also noted, bears some comparison with the ancient Jesus Prayer: "Lord Jesus Christ, Son of God, have mercy on me, a sinner." Its content, however, is arguably far closer to the prayer that people will find most familiar from the Stations of the Cross: "Save us, savior of the world, for by your Cross and Resurrection, you have set us free." Save *us*.

This first person plural (we, our) orientation is one that the Fátima prayer shares with what are, surely, the two most-prayed prayers within the Catholic Tradition. The Lord's Prayer, as we've already mentioned, asks that "*Our* Father...forgive *us our* trespasses [and] deliver *us* from evil."[17] The Hail Mary entreats the Mother of God to "pray for *us* sinners, now and at the hour of *our* death." The Lord's Prayer has, since the Church's early days, been often described as "a summary of the whole Gospel."[18] Likewise, the biblical richness of the Hail Mary—its first half mainly consists of two direct quotations from Luke (1:28, 43)[19]—has frequently been noted. Given the richness and depth of the Gospel, I do not wish to claim that the Fátima Prayer's twenty-nine words offer a complete précis. Though, as we have noted, it certainly does include many of the key themes. An orientation to, and for, others—and a deep concern for their eternal fate—is yet another instance of this.

REFLECTION QUESTIONS

1. At Fátima, Our Lady was very clear that hell was real, and wanted to save souls from ending up there. When was the last time I really considered this reality? How can I take Mary's words, and this part of the prayer, as a motivation for my spiritual life?

2. Pope Francis preaches often, especially in his daily Mass homilies, about the reality of the devil and of hell, but also speaks often of God's mercy. In the context of the New Evangelization, how can we create a good balance between raising awareness of the reality of hell, but yet not sinking into despair?

3. Often, hell is thought of as a punishment only for personal sins, but the *Catechism* also notes that hell is a possible punishment for our failings toward others (*CCC* 1033). How does the Fátima Prayer make us aware of both personal and social sins?

4

And lead all souls to heaven

*G*iven the previous chapter, the Fátima Prayer cannot be accused of soft-peddling the doctrine of hell, ultimately because Jesus himself did not. All too often, one meets with claims such that the doctrine of hell is unworthy of our Lord, or inimical to the overall thrust of his teaching. But these breezy assertions contradict Jesus' own words (see Luke 13:22–30). Speaking personally, it is far easier to imagine myself being ultimately confined to "those hidden abodes, in which are detained the souls that have not obtained heavenly bliss"[1] than I can other people. I know my own failings: those many times when I am neither hot nor cold, but lukewarm (Rev 3:15–16); when I have neglected Christ in the least of his brethren (Matt 25:31–44); when "I do not do what I want, but I do the very thing I hate"

(Rom 7:15). And I am very mindful of Vatican II's stern cautioning:

> All the Church's children should remember that their exalted status is to be attributed not to their own merits but to the special grace of Christ. If they fail moreover to respond to that grace in thought, word and deed, not only shall they not be saved but they will be the more severely judged. (*Lumen Gentium* 14)

But as to other people…well, "Who am I to judge?"

Jesus *also* says that "God did not send the Son into the world to condemn the world, but in order that the world might be saved through him" (John 3:17). Elsewhere, he promises, "I, when I am lifted up from the earth, will draw all people to myself" (John 12:32). Paul tells us that God "desires everyone to be saved and to come to the knowledge of the truth" (1 Tim 2:4). And as he quotes from Isaiah: "As I live, says the Lord, every knee shall bow to me, / and every tongue shall give praise to God" (Rom 14:11, quoting Isa 45:23; see also Phil 2:10).

What on earth—or more to the point, what in heaven—is going on here? The difficulty of these texts, which seem to at least allow the possibility of everyone ultimately being saved, becomes clear when looked at side-by-side with texts we discussed in the last chapter. And it is a difficulty that has been recognized since ancient times. According to St. Augustine, for example: We must inquire in what sense is said of God what the apostle has mostly truly said: "Who will have all men to be saved" (1 Timothy 2:4). For, as a matter of fact, not all, nor even a majority, are saved: so that it would seem that what God wills is not done, man's will interfering with, and hindering the will of God.[2]

Augustine's own solution, incidentally, is to suppose that the passage cannot really mean what it says after all: either it simply means that each person who is saved is so because God wills it, or "all men" is just a quick way of saying "all sorts of men."[3] Such interpretative gerrymandering has not, however, found universal favor within the Church's Tradition.

St. Thomas Aquinas, for instance, is quite plain that God really does will that all people be saved, even if not all people end up being saved.[4] Nevertheless, this is a huge and longstanding topic, and here is neither the time nor the place to try to resolve it. This is, lest we forget, just a short book on a prayer of (in English) only twenty-nine words.

Five of those words are, however, very much to the point here: *Lead all souls to heaven*. Since we refused to shy away from the full force of the previous clause's mention of "the fires of hell," we must do the same for this clause, evincing a *hope* that *all* may be saved.

The fact that this is indeed the plain meaning of the words, as they have been given to us, is clear. Interestingly, they seem to have struck some people as problematic since fairly early on. In 1946, for instance, Sr. Lucia had to correct versions of the prayer that had the phrase "have mercy on the souls in purgatory" in place of the more radical-sounding original.[5]

In his famous book *Dare We Hope that "All Men Be Saved"?*, Hans Urs von Balthasar argues that we are indeed permitted to hope.[6] His basic contention is that, as noted above, Scripture presents us with two, seemingly contradictory, sets of statements on the subject. It is not, he points out, for mere humans to adjudicate between the two: how the tension will ultimately be solved is God's problem, not ours. And that, for von Balthasar, allows us to *hope* that all, somehow, may indeed be saved. More recently, the same basic argument has also been made by the evangelical pastor Rob Bell in his 2012 bestseller *Love Wins*.[7] Writing in response to these views, Bishop Robert Barron observed,

> We don't know for sure. We are in fact permitted to hope and pray that all people will finally surrender to the alluring beauty of God's grace....We may, indeed we should, hope that God's grace will, in the end, wear down even the most recalcitrant sinner.[8]

Another layer to the question of universalism is a passage from Vatican II's *Lumen Gentium*. In paragraph 16, the Council Fathers note the possibility of salvation for those who lived before Christ lived (i.e., the Old Testament prophets), for the Jewish people, Muslims, extending even to those who don't know God, but live according to the dictates of their conscience, cooperating with grace. Needless to say, this is a wide scope, and perhaps justifies a hope that many can possibly be saved. Yet, the Fathers also note that "often," men (and one might assume, women, too) can easily be deceived when trying to strive for truth and goodness without the assistance of the Church. In any event, the Church seems to boldly proclaim that we ought to hope for, and in the context of this prayer, *pray* for the salvation of all. It's possible, and that alone should give us all great hope.

With some sense of the scope of the *hope* that is at work in this prayer, we might do well, just as we did in the previous chapter, to consider what it is that we know about heaven. The *Catechism* notes that heaven means "to be with Christ" and that this state of being is the "fulfillment of the deepest human longings" (*CCC* 1024). That is, of course, a fine theological definition, but what does it mean to "be with Christ" in a definitive state? To what can we compare this? Surely, this reality must be so sublime that no mere words could ever truly describe it. Still, there are plenty of words used to try and give us some sense of what heaven will be like.

For example, we are told that heaven will be like a house with many rooms and that Jesus will go there and prepare a room for us (John 14:1–3). In another work by the same author, we read that heaven will be like a "marriage supper of the Lamb" (Rev 19:9). St. Matthew's Gospel also gives us the image of a wedding feast to which many are invited, but few respond. Out of frustration, the host tells his servants to invite anyone he can, but those who are wearing the wrong garment are cast out (Matt 22:1–14). This is a helpful parable, as it gives us an image of the *desire* for God to save many, or invite many of us to his wedding feast. The problem is that many of us reject that invitation.

It may be helpful to recall what we said above: these are images, analogies, metaphors; that is, heaven will not really be any of those things. We can say that there will be even *more* dissimilarity between the images of heaven and the reality than there will be between the images of hell and its reality. We should also recall that it is wise not to take any depiction of heaven as the definitive final word. There is a healthy sense of mystery about eternal beatitude. A browse through the *Catechism*, encyclicals, the writings of the ecumenical councils, and other official documents will reveal scant descriptions of heaven. That's part of the plan of God, and we do well to retain a healthy sense of mystery and intrigue. Furthermore, the images from Scripture also provide us with some sense of heaven.

A significant key to understanding the image of heaven is revealed in the Mass, which is referred to as the *heavenly* liturgy for a reason: at the Mass, we participate in the liturgy of heaven. The Book of Revelation, when examined closely, shows a stunning similarity to the liturgy of the Mass: scrolls that can only be read by certain people, liturgical chant, incense, the sacrifice of the Lamb, and chalices.[9] A further aspect should be mentioned here, too. Both in the beatitude of heaven, as well as in the liturgy of the Mass, we are united with the Communion of Saints. That is, we are worshipping together and in union with all those who have gone before us marked with the sign of faith, both the canonized giants like St. Augustine, St. John Paul II, and Thérèse of Lisieux, as well as all of the unknown, humble souls who are known to God alone. Thus, just as the Fátima Prayer unites the horizontal and vertical dimensions of spirituality, so too the Church's teachings on heaven help us to realize that we will experience (and are already getting a foretaste at the Mass) eternal beatitude not *just* as individuals, but also as part of a union with others. In heaven as on earth, we pray not just for ourselves, but also for others.

This stirring vision of hope is certainly attractive. Indeed, faith, hope, and charity are at the very heart of Fátima. The current *Catechism* speaks of "God's universal plan of salvation," stating that "God 'desires all men to be saved and to come to the knowledge of the truth'; that is, God wills the salvation of everyone through the knowledge of the truth" (*CCC* 851).

REFLECTION QUESTIONS

1. In the contemporary world, it's easy to hunker down and retreat into a sort of Catholic ghetto mentality. How can we grow as disciples by praying not only for our own salvation and entrance into heaven, but even that "all souls" might be led there?

2. How can praying this part of the Fátima Prayer help us to heal wounds with those who have hurt us, whether they are family members, coworkers, friends, or enemies?

3. Which images are more difficult for me to grapple with: the images of the "fires of hell" or the descriptions of heaven in Scripture and the *Catechism* (nos. 1023–29)? Why?

4. Do I consider the communal dimension of heaven in my own spiritual life and prayer? How might I take strength and encouragement from those who have already reached heaven, both in Mass and in my own devotional and prayer life?

5

Especially those in most need of thy mercy

*I*n order to better appreciate this line, it is helpful to split it into two parts. First, we will focus on what it means to pray for those "especially in most need" of God's mercy; and second, we will dwell more on the significance of this mercy, of which so many are in need.

Many people may consider the message of Fátima as being mostly a prognosis of bad news. There were, after all, plenty of dire warnings given to the children: people are going astray, nobody is praying the Rosary, and war is coming if things don't change. But in the Fátima Prayer, we have Mary, the very Mother of God (*Theotokos*), telling us to pray so that those in most need of mercy might go to heaven. This aspect of the Fátima Prayer, imploring mercy on "those in most need" is powerful, and also challenging.

First, who precisely *is* in "most need"? It might be our first thought that it's those horrible sinners about whom we hear so much: public sinners whose scandals fill the news headlines, all those lazy Catholics who don't go to Mass, and so on. But if we take this route, we might begin to sound suspiciously like a certain Pharisee who uttered this prayer:

> God, I thank you that I am not like other people: thieves, rogues, adulterers, or even like this tax collector. I fast twice a week; I give a tenth of all my income. (Luke 18:11–12)

The Pharisee, in his pride and hardness of heart, had forgotten a critical point that he, too, was a sinner. While the Pharisee may be more familiar to us, Graham Greene has an interesting take on this idea as well. In his *Power and the Glory*, the Whiskey Priest winds up in a jail cell where he overhears a pious woman accuse some of her cellmates of being brutes and animals, but doesn't accuse *herself*. The priest responds by saying, "It needs a lot of learning to see things with a saint's eye: a saint gets a subtle taste for beauty and can look down on poor ignorant palates like theirs. But we can't afford to."[1] This is, more or less, the same message of the parable from Luke's Gospel.

If the sin in Luke's parable is having an overly high estimation of our own virtue, and thus a low estimation of our need for mercy, the remedy is an honest self-knowledge. His prayer is contrasted with the tax collector whose simple prayer was remarkably similar to the current line of the Fátima Prayer we are considering:

God, be merciful to me, a sinner! (Luke 18:13)

The answer to the question of who is in "most need" of God's mercy is, well, me. It's us. We are *all* in great need of mercy. To help us recall that, the Church has been on a veritable mission of mercy lately, most notably with the recent Jubilee Year of Mercy.

In his official proclamation of the Jubilee, Pope Francis extolled the Lord Jesus as the "face of mercy" (*Misericordiae Vultus*). In the letter, he recounts, in his inimitable style, the way God has revealed himself, both in the Old and New Testaments, to be a God full of mercy. Indeed, God himself makes known to Moses that he is a Lord "slow to anger, and abounding in steadfast love and faithfulness" (Exod 34:6). But especially through the life of Jesus Christ, we see mercy extend itself explicitly as he suffers for the least, the last, and those who might not even know that they are in need of mercy. Significantly, it is those who are unaware of their need for mercy that are in most danger. Conversely, those who are most aware of their need for mercy are probably the least in need of it.

For example, examine the life of any saint, especially those who have left journals or diaries, and one immediately comes to the very counterintuitive realization that it is these holy men and women who are most painfully aware of their sinfulness and their need for mercy. Part of the challenge of this part of the prayer is realizing that it is *us* who are in so great a need of mercy. Two modern examples will make this clear.

In the late 1800s, Thérèse of Lisieux pursued radical holiness through her Little Way, and under obedience to her superior (and her real-life sister), she penned her famous *The Story of a Soul*, which has been translated into multiple languages. For me, her story was initially very puzzling, for I knew that this woman was a Doctor of the Church and that she was called the "greatest saint of modern times" by Pope Pius X. But upon reading her journal, I realized that she didn't think very highly of herself.

Of course, one should immediately be suspect of anyone boldly proclaiming their own sanctity. But Thérèse's brutal honesty and blunt self-assessment can be shocking. It was not, however, the result of some sort of psychological insecurity or false humility. Instead, her honesty and humility was due to a deep and personal relationship with Jesus. Because she was aware of the sublime beauty of Christ's own self-sacrifice, she was more keenly aware of just how little she could offer in comparison. Deep in her heart, she knew that she was a small soul, called to the simplicity of trust in Jesus. In fact, when her spiritual director declared that she had never committed a single mortal sin in her life, she notes that he said this was a grace that was given to her, "without any merit on her part." Rather than being insulted or defensive about this, she writes,

Without any merit on my part! That was not difficult to believe. I knew how very weak I was and how imperfect. My heart overflowed with gratitude.[2]

In Thérèse's journal, one reads time and time again of moments of honest simplicity, like that of a child. She is a simple soul, and she thanks God for it. She prays, she follows the rule of her community, and she sometimes annoys an old nun she was told to care for. There is no effort to make herself seem great, because she knows she's not, and that is precisely the point of the spiritual life.[3] But when she looks at herself, she doesn't see merely herself; she looks past her own reflection and gazes at Christ, the only one truly capable of perfection. She sees in him the solution to all of her problems, the one who can take her exactly as she is, as a child in his hands, and bring her close to his heart. As she describes it,

> This Little flower, in telling her story, is happy to make known all the gifts that Jesus has given to her. She knows quite well that He could not have been attracted by anything she had of her own. Purely out of mercy He gave these gifts.[4]

It is this self-awareness, this simplicity of being, that allowed Thérèse to be attuned to the graces God had in store for her. It is also this attitude of radical simplicity that makes the most sense of mercy. The moment we begin to feel our own self-sufficiency, or explain away our failings, we are immediately in danger of turning away from the radical gift of God's mercy. Thérèse's method of small sacrifices and radical dependence on God is, I daresay, more needed today than it was in her lifetime.

Another example of radical awareness of the need for mercy comes from the life of Venerable Fulton Sheen. In his autobiography, Sheen shares stories that give us an insight into his personal life, providing all sorts of interesting details about his education, his life's work in radio and television, his gift for speaking, and more. One story he tells, though, speaks powerfully about the consciousness that a saint (or a venerable) has of their own shortcomings. The story concerns one of his trips "in the missions" where he was paying a visit to a leper colony in Africa. According to Sheen, he brought with him a small gift for each of the lepers: a small silver crucifix. When it was time to hand them out, he caught sight of the first leper's condition and hesitated. Rather than handing the crucifix to the man, he dropped it. To most of us that may seem an ordinary way to respond, especially if we've never met someone suffering from leprosy before. But for Sheen, the hesitation in the sight of this leper was shameful. He says of the moment,

> All of a sudden there were 501 lepers in that camp; I was the 501st because I had taken that symbol of God's identification with man and refused to identify myself with someone who was a thousand times better on the

inside than I. Then it came over me the awful thing I had done. I dug my fingers into his leprosy, took out the crucifix and pressed it into his hand. And so on, for all the other 499 lepers. From that moment on I learned to love them.[5]

Both Bishop Sheen and St. Thérèse have much to teach the contemporary world. We're very much pressured into believing that we're okay, that things are okay and, certainly, that there's nothing wrong with us. How often do you hear people talk about how they have no regrets, as if this is a tremendous accomplishment? For a saint (or a venerable), there are regrets, but ones that are healed by Christ's mercy. Let us now consider the significance of this mercy for the children of Fátima and the world.

The apparitions at Fátima revealed that a terrible struggle was coming not only for the Church, but indeed for the whole world if Our Lady's directives were not followed. She asked, of course, for the prayer of the Rosary, the devotion of first Saturdays, and the consecration of Russia, and noted that if these things did not happen, Russia would infect the world with its errors and that an even worse war would soon come. Recall again that the Fátima Prayer was revealed after a glimpse into hell. According to the record, things were not looking particularly good for the future; yet, in the midst of this, the children were taught to implore God's mercy.

As time passed, it was evident that the instructions given at Fátima were perhaps not followed. There were a few attempts at a consecration of Russia, but never with a wide participation. In fact, Pope Pius XII did consecrate the world to the Immaculate Heart in October 1942, and a second time in December 1942. Of course, by then, World War II was already well under way. It's in this context that we can now appreciate the connection between the message of Fátima and the message of Divine Mercy.

While the apparitions at Fátima asked people to pray for God's mercy in order to avert greater evil, the message of Divine Mercy is revealed in the midst of this terrible evil. In the context of a world that was falling apart and in which the West clearly seemed to lose any and all sense of sin, Jesus appeared, once again, to a humble and simple soul and revealed the depths of his mercy.

Saint Faustina, born Mary Faustina Kowalska, was from a poor family in Poland, where she lived an almost entirely hidden existence. She attended school for only three years and worked as a housekeeper before finally entering religious life at the age of twenty. (She had asked for her parents' permission earlier in life but was denied.) During her time in the convent, there was nothing extraordinary about her life. She worked at simple tasks and, to those around her, seemed a normal religious sister. But within her spiritual life, she was experiencing tremendous gifts including "revelations, visions, hidden stigmata, participation in the Passion of the Lord, the gift of bilocation, the reading of human souls, the gift of prophecy, or the rare gift of mystical engagement and marriage."[6]

Yet, as Faustina rightly realized, these tremendous spiritual gifts were only accessories, or ornaments. Her true vocation lay not in the extraordinary spiritual experiences she was having, but in her mission as a messenger of Divine Mercy. In fact, in her *Diary* she records God telling her that in the Old Testament, he sent prophets, but now (in the twentieth century), he was sending her.[7] The mission, which was recorded in her *Diary* at Jesus' own wish, as well as with the permission of her spiritual director, consisted primarily of three items:

1. Preaching the message of Jesus' truly unending mercy for all souls;
2. Promoting the Divine Mercy Chaplet, the prayer at the hour of mercy (3:00 p.m.), and making known Jesus' desire for the Feast of Divine Mercy; and
3. Initiating a movement of Divine Mercy within the Church.

While Sister Faustina was faithful to the visions and recorded what she was asked to in her *Diary*, there's a sense in which the mission entrusted to her was too much. But might this not be the normal way that God operates: by asking too much of us? In one of her visions, Faustina sees the Pope celebrating what seems to be the Feast of Divine Mercy, but she isn't sure how it could come to pass.[8] For the Divine Mercy message to get out, it seemed that the world would need a messenger with a wider audience than this simple Polish nun.

Of course, Sister Faustina would die before the Feast of Divine Mercy would be celebrated by the universal Church. But St. John Paul II seemed keenly aware that the message of Divine Mercy was of major importance for the world. That's why, along with the canonization of St. Faustina on Divine Mercy Sunday in the Jubilee year of 2000, John Paul II opened up the feast to the whole Church, completing the vision of St. Faustina. The Feast of Divine Mercy, if we prepare for it according to the instructions in the *Diary* of St. Faustina, is the true answer to the evil in the world. Where the message of Fátima proclaimed that we entreat God's mercy to prevent future evil, the message of Divine Mercy through St. Faustina taught us that we can also erase the evil of our past.

One can certainly say, then, that the Fátima Prayer leads us to the arms of Divine Mercy. In the midst of World War I, Our Lady appeared, asking us to entreat God's mercy to prevent a future and greater war. When World War II arrived, Sister Faustina was already learning the message of Divine Mercy. And finally, when a man who lived through the atrocities of the Nazis and the Communists was called to the chair of St. Peter, there was a new birth of mercy, a new opportunity. The prayer of Fátima is still valid, even though the secret has been revealed and time has passed. The mercy of God never expires, and in this brief stanza of the prayer—"especially those in most need of thy mercy"—we are being prepared for and reminded of the message of Divine Mercy. People often group together the Our Father, the Hail Mary, and the Glory Be as a classic trio of Catholic prayers. We might also pray a Catholic duet of prayers: the Fátima Prayer and Faustina's famous prayer: "Jesus, I trust in you."

REFLECTION QUESTIONS

1. How easily do I forget that I am in need of God's mercy? How can the Fátima Prayer help me to remember my dependence on God, and his providential care for me?
2. In this period of the Church, there has been increasing emphasis on God's mercy. How can I take the Church's message and bring mercy into my personal spiritual life, and more importantly, into my family's life? How can an appreciation of God's mercy on *me* lead me to be more merciful to *others*?
3. Have I trusted fully in God's mercy and tried to take advantage of some of the opportunities that the Church gives us to encounter the Divine Mercy? If not, why?

6

Amen

*R*egarding the final word of the Fátima Prayer, it may seem strange to write an entire chapter, however brief, on the meaning of a single word. In fact, the uttering of "amen," however mindlessly it might take place, actually has deep significance. To say "amen," moreover, without taking note of what we are truly saying amen *in response to*, is a very common, but nonetheless real, sin of omission. How can that be?

We would do well to realize the way that the Church thinks of the word *amen*. As any good, or even lukewarm, Catholic would know, we always use the word *amen* at the end of prayers. We recite this word, usually pretty mechanically, at the end of the Sign of the Cross, the Our Father, the Hail Mary, and just about any prayer you can think of. The word *amen* is also one of the easiest words to teach children when they're learning their prayers. At least, my little ones have always found it easy to say.

Interestingly, it's also the last word of the Bible, and, while not the actual last word, it is also the final subject that the *Catechism* discusses. The "amen" is also sung boldly in the Mass as the "Great Amen" at the climax of the Eucharistic Prayer. Thus, quite obviously, the word *amen* has great significance if for no other reason than that we say it so often! But why do we say it so much?

In the language of the *Catechism*, the "amen" takes the role of a ratifying clause that, in a certain way, reaffirms and solidifies what we have just stated (*CCC* 2856).[1] Earlier on, in the discussion of the Creed, the *Catechism* notes that "in Hebrew, amen comes from the same root as the word 'believe'" (*CCC* 1062).[2] Thus, the meaning of our frequent recourse to this word after all of our prayers is to reaffirm what we have just stated. Put simply, one might say that *amen* means "Yes, I believe." *Amen* has to do with the truth of what has been stated. In this way, Jesus uses the word often to emphasize the message he is preaching. He begins many of his stories by saying, "Amen, amen, I say to you." In many Bible translations, this is written as "Truly, truly, I say to you."[3]

Repetition of a word or phrase can sometimes be understood as watering down its meaning. People often say that "familiarity breeds contempt." And if that were true, maybe we ought to say "amen" less often, so that it means more every time we utter the word. But to do so would be to overlook another dimension of prayer and of the spiritual life. A helpful analogy is to think of human relationships like marriage and parenting. These are situations in which repetition is *unavoidable*. You will repeat yourself both in the words you use and the actions you must undertake: hugs, wiping tears, changing diapers, preparing meals, cutting up food, doing laundry, and the like. All of these actions seem to go on interminably, repeating themselves for decades. So, too, will some of the words that form an important part of relationships: "I'm sorry," "I forgive you," and most poignantly, "I love you" (cf. John 21:15–19).

So, while we are perhaps not always paying attention to the deep meaning of the "amen" at the end of each prayer, we need not throw the baby out with the bathwater. We should remind ourselves that it means we trust and believe in the prayer we have just said. In a similar context, St. John Paul II reminded us that the repetition involved in prayer must be understood properly. Instead of mechanical and mindless thought, John Paul II suggests that the repeated prayers of the Christian life should be seen more as an "outpouring of that love which tirelessly returns to the person loved with expressions similar in their content but ever fresh in terms of the feeling pervading them" (*Rosarium Virginis Mariae* 26).

Now, with some sense of what we are saying when we pray the word *amen*, let us now consider the entire Fátima Prayer:

> *O my Jesus,*
> *Forgive us our sins.*
> *Save us from the fires of hell,*
> *And lead all souls to heaven*
> *Especially those in most need of thy mercy.*
> *Amen*

Affirming the "amen" in this prayer, we are recapitulating all that has come before it. First, this prayer has us claiming a seriously personal relationship with Jesus, modeled on the relationship he has with Mary. We use the language of children to call Jesus "my Jesus." Immediately after this endearing address, we ask him to forgive *us* of *our* sins, expanding from a mere personal concern and relationship into a concern for others. We ask to be delivered from hell, remembering the vision given to the children of what torment might await those who didn't follow Mary's requests, and also holding firm to Jesus' clear and very uncomfortable words about Gehenna. Then, we immediately ask and hope that somehow all of us might go to heaven, exhibiting great trust in Jesus. In particular, though, we ask those in most need of mercy to be led to the eternal beatitude we call heaven. After having uttered these words, trustingly and solemnly we proclaim, "Amen."

Appendix

Praying the Rosary

*S*t. John Paul II declared 2002 the Year of the Rosary to encourage the faithful to pray the Rosary both more often and with a more attentive heart. To launch the Year of the Rosary and to make the prayer of the Rosary more effective, he wrote the letter titled *Rosarium Virginis Mariae*. In that short letter, the Pope offers a poignant reflection on what he called his favorite prayer. Since the Fátima Prayer was revealed in the context of apparitions, in which Mary entreated the faithful to pray the Rosary every day, and indeed since she asked for the Fátima Prayer to be included after each mystery of the Rosary, it is helpful to note some of John Paul's advice on the Rosary. While the entire letter covers a wide range of topics about praying, we will focus here mostly on the last section of the letter in which he offers his insights on how to pray the Rosary more effectively. It is, in a sense, a lesson from a spiritual master on how to approach this great prayer.

LISTENING TO THE WORD OF GOD

One of John Paul's suggestions is that, following the announcement of the mystery being prayed, we should read a related biblical passage. So, for instance, in the prayer of the first joyful mystery, we might read through St. Luke's account of the Annunciation as an aid to our prayer. Depending on the circumstances—that is, a private prayer of the Rosary versus a parish-wide gathering—the reading could be shorter or longer; it may even be appropriate to read a brief commentary on the reading before moving on to pray and contemplate the mystery. This also helps us break up the auto-pilot of simply rushing through the prayers. As John Paul says, "It is not a matter of recalling information but of allowing God to speak" (*Rosarium Virginis Mariae* 30).

SILENCE

Early on in the letter, St. John Paul II tells us that praying the Rosary means following the example of Mary. What he has in mind here is imitating her as a disciple, or enrolling in the "school of Mary" (no. 1). We should recall that "Mary treasured all these words and pondered them in her heart" (Luke 2:19). That is, she meditated, contemplated, and deeply considered the reality of her life and her vocation, as well as her Son's mission. In other words, she was an expert at practicing silence. As John Paul notes, "Listening and meditation are nourished by silence" (no. 31). Noting the connection between the Rosary and the liturgy, he points out that, just as we pause in the liturgy for silence, it is fitting to do so in the prayer of the Rosary as well. What does that mean for us? Certainly, it means we can't, and shouldn't, rush straight through from one prayer to the next. We should pause and listen after the announcement of the mystery, perhaps, or after the reading, if we're able to include a reading. At the very least, we should pause *somewhere* to be still and listen. We might recall here the fact that God can't always be heard in the midst of the great noise of life's storms, but his voice is often found in the "sound of sheer silence" (1 Kings 19:12).

THE HAIL MARY

As we noted earlier, the Hail Mary is an eminently biblical prayer. In *Rosarium Virginis Mariae*, John Paul shows us that while of course most of the text of this prayer comes from the gospel, there is also a certain reverberation with the text of Genesis. The words of the Angel Gabriel, according to John Paul, express adoration of the mystery of the Incarnation. Here, we find a parallel between the angel's greetings and God's proclamation in Genesis that creation was "good." The Hail Mary helps us share in that "jubilant amazement" as we acknowledge the greatest miracle of history" (no. 33).

Discussing the Hail Mary, John Paul II has a powerful reminder for us: the word "Jesus" is the "center of gravity of this prayer," and we should emphasize it. One way to emphasize this, he suggests, is to pause after the mention of the name (another moment of silence), and before completing the prayer. Furthermore, he suggests the addition of a clause referring to the mystery being contemplated. This can be a great aid in keeping our focus on the mystery being contemplated, as it would repeat our reference to the mystery ten times! For instance, if the mystery is the "Carrying of the Cross," we could pray,

Hail Mary, full of grace,
the Lord is with thee.
Blessed art thou among women,
and blessed is the fruit of thy womb, Jesus,
who carried the cross.

THE GLORY BE

After the recitation of the Hail Mary, John Paul II gives us another recommendation that can help to enrich the contemplation of our prayer. The Gloria is, after all, an explicitly Trinitarian prayer, and it ought to be the high point of our contemplation. John Paul, who was quite a singer in his time, suggests that in order to prevent this, we should *sing* the Glory Be as a way to give it special emphasis and keep it from becoming a mere afterthought.

CONCLUDING PRAYER

After the Glory Be, of course, is the Fátima Prayer, which we have already considered at length. Yet John Paul II also has another suggestion. In his view, we could make our Rosary more contemplative by following each decade with a prayer asking for the fruits of that specific mystery. Here's a list of the fruits of the mysteries:

THE JOYFUL MYSTERIES
1. The Annunciation—Humility
2. The Visitation—Love of Neighbor
3. The Nativity of the Lord—Poverty of Spirit, Detachment from Worldly Things
4. Presentation—Obedience
5. Finding of the Child Jesus in the Temple—Piety

THE LUMINOUS MYSTERIES
1. The Baptism of Jesus—Openness to the Holy Spirit
2. The Miracle at Cana—To Jesus through Mary
3. Proclamation of the Kingdom of God—Repentance, Trust in God
4. Transfiguration—Desire for Holiness
5. Institution of the Eucharist—Eucharistic Adoration, Participation at Mass

SORROWFUL MYSTERIES
1. Agony in the Garden—Contrition, Conformity to the Will of God

2. Scourging at the Pillar—Purity, Mortification
3. Crowning with Thorns—Moral Courage
4. Carrying of the Cross—Patience
5. Crucifixion—Salvation, Self-Denial

GLORIOUS MYSTERIES
1. The Resurrection—Faith
2. The Ascension—Hope, Desire for Heaven
3. The Descent of the Holy Spirit—Wisdom, Love of God
4. The Assumption of Mary—Devotion to Mary
5. The Coronation of the Blessed Virgin Mary— Eternal Happiness

FREQUENCY OF PRAYING THE ROSARY

Though John Paul II doesn't say so explicitly, he certainly implies that the ideal is to pray the entire Rosary every day. However, he notes that may not be possible, especially with the addition of the Luminous Mysteries.

As an alternative, he suggests that we can pray one set of mysteries per day, and that this will give each day of the week a certain "color," much like the liturgical seasons of the year give us a specific character. It also can give shape to our entire week:

In the Rosary, in a way similar to what takes place in the liturgy, the Christian week, centered on Sunday, the day of resurrection, becomes a journey through the mysteries of the life of Christ." (no. 38)

Thus, the practice of praying the Sorrowful Mysteries on Tuesdays and Fridays, the Joyful on Monday and Saturday, the Glorious on Wednesday and Sunday, and the Luminous on Thursdays gives our week a liturgical structure.

THE ROSARY AND THE FAMILY

John Paul II strongly recommends that families make a concerted effort to pray the Rosary daily and says that the Rosary is, and always has been "a prayer of and for the family." Many of us may be familiar with the worldwide Family Rosary Crusade of the 1950s that eventually became a Roman Catholic movement founded by Patrick Peyton, an Irish-American priest, who is being considered for sainthood by the Vatican for his efforts in encouraging families to pray the Rosary. John Paul mentions this heritage, which unfortunately is more of a record of history than a living memory, and encourages all families to reclaim this great tradition of prayer.

Aside from the richness of praying the Rosary, a family praying the Rosary must also create time to be together; time to focus on what is most important. If you make time for the Rosary or any other prayer, for that matter, you will be providing your family with something meaningful and important, not just entertainment and idle time. As he notes,

Families seldom manage to come together, and the rare occasions when they do are often taken up with watching television. To return to the recitation of the family Rosary means filling daily life with very different images, images of the mystery of salvation: the image of the Redeemer, the image of his most Blessed Mother. The family that recites the Rosary together reproduces something of the atmosphere of the household of Nazareth: its members place Jesus at the center. (no. 41)

Finally, especially remembering that the Fátima Prayer and the apparitions were gifts given to the Church through the mediation of three children aged ten and under, let us consider how John Paul II understood the relationship between the Rosary and children. Even Jacinta, Francisco, and Lucia didn't always have the patience to pray through a whole Rosary, as we discussed earlier. So what are the Pope's thoughts about the reality or possibility of children praying the Rosary?

First, he states that a daily pause for prayer, while not being a solution to every problem, is "a spiritual aid which should not be underestimated" (no. 42). Of course, he is aware that many people argue that the Rosary is not suited for children, especially today's youth. He replies that perhaps they have never seen the Rosary prayed well, or prayed in a manner that would actually help them understand the mysteries and lead them to authentic contemplation. And then he issues perhaps the best line of the whole letter: "Why not try it?"

After all, World Youth Day gives us pretty good evidence that the traditional marks of Catholicism are not the problem; perhaps we don't trust young people enough. The Pope says that if we give the Rosary a chance, he is quite sure that "young people will once more surprise adults by the way they make this prayer their own and recite it with the enthusiasm typical of their age group" (no. 42).

Notes

PREFACE

1. *The Salvation of Atheists and Catholic Dogmatic Theology* (Oxford: Oxford University Press, 2012), 186; *Faith and Unbelief* (London: Canterbury Press, 2013; Mahwah, NJ: Paulist Press, 2014), 90.

2. Alistair Stewart-Sykes, trans. and ed., *Tertullian, Origen and Cyprian on The Lord's Prayer* (New York: St. Vladimir's Seminary Press, 2004); Scott Hahn, *Understanding "Our Father": Biblical Reflections on the Lord's Prayer* (Steubenville, OH: Emmaus Road, 2002).

3. For reasons of style, we have retained the use of *I* and *my* throughout, without specifying to which of us they belong, when relating a personal impression or anecdote.

INTRODUCTION

1. Of course, Pacelli would later become known as Pope Pius XII.

2. Pope John Paul II, "Beatification Homily of Jacinta and Francisco." See https://w2.vatican.va/content/john-paul-ii/en/travels/2000/documents/hf_jp-ii_hom_20000513_beatification-fatima.html.

3. William Thomas Walsh, *Our Lady of Fátima* (New York: Image Books, 1990), 22.

4. Ibid., 36.

5. Ibid., 42.

6. Lucia Santos, *Fatima in Sister Lucia's Own Words* (Still River, MA: Ravengate Press, 1974), 174.

7. Ibid., 175.

8. Ibid.

9. For a more detailed description of the vision, see The Congregation for the Doctrine of Faith, "The Message of Fatima," http://www.vatican.va/roman_curia/congregations/cfaith/documents/rc_con_cfaith_doc_20000626_message-fatima_en.html.

10. Santos, *Fatima in Sister Lucia's Own Words*, 179.

11. Michael E. Gaitley, MIC, *The Second Greatest Story Ever Told* (Stockbridge, MA: Marian Press, 2015), 99–103.

12. Joseph Ratzinger, "The Message of Fatima," in *Fatima in Sister Lucia's Own Words*, 215. See also http://www.vatican.va/roman_curia/congregations/cfaith/documents/rc_con_cfaith_doc_20000626_message-fatima_en.html.

13. Pope John Paul II, *Memory and Identity* (New York: Rizzoli, 2005), 159.

14. Announcement made by Cardinal Angelo Sodano, "The Message of Fatima," in *Fatima in Sister Lucia's Own Words*, 219.

15. Santos, *Fatima in Sister Lucia's Own Words*, 220.

16. Joseph Ratzinger, "The Message of Fatima," in *Fatima in Sister Lucia's Own Words*, 224.

CHAPTER 1

1. Eusebius of Caesarea, *Proof of the Gospel*, IV, 6.

2. Fulton J. Sheen, *The Last Seven Words* (New York: Alba House, 1996), 17.

3. Irenaeus of Lyons, *The Demonstration of Apostolic Preaching*, trans. Armitage Robinson (London: SPCK, 1920), no. 75.

4. The *Catechism of the Catholic Church*, for instance, notes that the Jesus Prayer connects us with both the Christological hymn of Phil 2:6–11 as well as the prayer of the blind beggar. Thus, in the space of just a few words, we move from high theology to humble mercy. See *CCC*, no. 2667.

5. See St. John Paul II, Apostolic Letter, *Rosarium Virginis Mariae*, no. 12.

6. Sister Maria Lucia of Jesus, *Fatima in Lucia's Own Words: Sister Lucia's Memoirs*, ed. Louis Kondor, trans. Dominican Nuns of Perpetual Rosary, 19th ed. (Fundação Francisco e Jacinta Marto, 2014), 43–44. [NB: All further references to Sr. Lucia's own writings will be to this edition.]

7. Ibid., 77.

8. Pope St. Leo the Great, *Sermon 55* (On the Lord's Passion, IV).

9. Pope St. John Paul II, General Audience, "Mary: Model of the Church at Prayer," September 10, 1997, *L'Osservatore Romano*, September 17, 1997, https://www.ewtn.com/library/PAPALDOC/JP2BVM62.HTM.

CHAPTER 2

1. Quoted in Antonio Spadaro, "A Big Heart Open to God: The Exclusive Interview with Pope Francis," *America*,

September 30, 2013, http://americamagazine.org/pope
-interview.

2. Ibid.

3. "God has been murdered," as St. Melito, the second-century bishop of Sardis in modern-day Turkey, bracingly put it. See Melito of Sardis and Alistair Stewart-Sykes, *On Pascha: Melito of Sardis, Circa 190 AD*, Popular Patristics (New York: St. Vladimir's Seminary Press, 2001), 96.

4. Edward Pentin, "Pope Francis' Consecrating the World to Mary Culminates Fatima Celebration," *National Catholic Register*, October 15, 2015, see http://www.ncregister.com/daily-news/pope-francis-consecrating-the-world-to-mary-culminates-fatima-celebration/.

5. While the famous apparitions of Our Lady at Fátima occurred in 1917, the way was suitably prepared by three appearances of the self-proclaimed "Angel of Peace" in the spring, summer, and fall of 1916. For a full discussion of the significance of these, see Andrew Apostoli, *Fatima for Today: The Urgent Marian Message of Hope* (San Francisco: Ignatius Press, 2010), 20–42. Not insignificantly, the first such apparition occurred just after the children's post-lunch Rosary, possibly—Lucia informs us—prayed in the children's abbreviated form, as described in chapter 1, but as she notes, "I'm not sure whether we said it that day in the way I have already described (*Fatima in Lucia's Own Words*, 77)."

6. Ibid.

7. See Charles Dickens's wonderful 1849 novel *David Copperfield*.

8. Fyodor Dostoevsky, *The Brothers Karamazov*, trans. Richard Pevear and Larissa Volokhonsky (London: Vintage, [1880] 2004), 246.

9. Quoted in Spadaro, "A Big Heart Open to God."

10. Pope Francis, *The Name of God Is Mercy* (New York: Random House, 2016), 52.

11. Quoted in Spadaro, "A Big Heart Open to God."

12. See, for example, *Amoris Laetitia* (2016), art. 291.

13. "Radio Message of His Holiness Pius XII to Participants in the National Catechetical Congress of the United States in Boston," October 26, 1946, https://w2.vatican.va/content/pius-xii/en/speeches/1946/documents/hf_p-xii_spe_19461026_congresso-catechistico-naz.html.

14. See John Allen Jr., *A People of Hope* (New York: Image Books, 2012).

15. See the famous words of Blessed Paul VI: "Modern man listens more willingly to witnesses than to teachers, and if he does listen to teachers, it is because they are witnesses" (*Evangelii Nuntiandi* [1975], 41).

16. Lucia goes on to record that the woman happened, unbeknownst to the children, to overhear this exchange: "She told my mother, afterwards, that what Jacinta did, made such an impression on her, that she needed no other proof to make her believe in the reality of the apparitions; henceforth she would not only not insult us anymore, but would constantly ask us to pray to Our Lady, that her sins might be forgiven," *Fatima in Lucia's Own Words*, 56–57.

17. Ibid., 45–46, 93.

18. Thomas Aquinas, *Summa Theologiae*, IIa IIae, Q. 39, a. 9.

19. Ibid., 62.

20. *Sollicitudo Rei Socialis* (1987), art. 38.

CHAPTER 3

1. For example, Pew Research Center, *U.S. Public Becoming Less Religious* (November 3, 2015), 54, see http://www.pewforum.org/files/2015/11/201.11.03_RLS_II_full_report.pdf.

2. Come to think of it, I suppose that I am such a one myself. See Stephen Bullivant, *The Salvation of Atheists and Catholic Dogmatic Theology* (Oxford: Oxford University Press, 2012).

3. For a helpful rundown of the Synoptic texts (i.e., Matthew, Mark, and Luke), see Dale C. Allison, *Resurrecting Jesus: The Earliest Christian Tradition and Its Interpreters* (New York: Bloomsbury, 2005), 63–67.

4. It may be helpful to contrast Jesus' mission, which is the very mission of God, with that of Jake and Elwood Blues' mission that, while from God, was not the very mission *of* God.

5. Pope John Paul II, "Letter of the Holy Father to All the Priests of the Church for Holy Thursday 1986," *EWTN*, 1999, https://www.ewtn.com/library/PAPALDOC/JP2CUR.htm.

6. Pope Benedict XVI, "Letter Proclaiming a Year of Priests," http://w2.vatican.va/content/benedict-xvi/en/letters/2009/documents/hf_ben-xvi_let_20090616_anno-sacerdotale.html.

7. According to Newman and Stine, "*Three measures…* represents an enormous amount of flour, amounting to approximately 39.4 liters or 50 pounds. It is estimated that the bread baked from this amount of dough would be sufficient for more than one hundred persons" (Barclay M. Newman and Philip C. Stine, *A Handbook on the Gospel of Matthew* [New York: United Bible Societies, 1988], 426–27).

8. Allison, *Resurrecting Jesus*, 91–92.

9. *Fatima in Lucia's Own Words*, 45.

10. These words come from Cardinal Bertone's introduction to the Congregation for the Doctrine of the Faith's 2000 document "The Message of Fatima," which is helpfully included as an appendix to *Fatima in Lucia's Own Words*. See p. 199.

11. *Fatima in Lucia's Own Words*, 178.

12. Ibid., 123.

13. Lucia has left us two accounts, in the "Third Memoir" and "Fourth Memoir," both written in 1941 (see ibid., 123–24, 178–79).

14. Joseph Ratzinger, "Theological Commentary," in *Fatima in Lucia's Own Words*, 227.

15. Francis Johnston, *Fatima: The Great Sign* (Chulmleigh: Augustine Publishing Company, 1980), 82. Note especially Francisco's words to Lucia on receiving Communion are worth repeating: "Today I am happier than you are…for I have the hidden Jesus in my heart."

16. *Fatima in Lucia's Own Words*, 125. Note also that regarding Jacinta, Lucia recalls, "The vision of hell filled her with horror to such a degree, that every penance and mortification was as nothing in her eyes, if only she could prevent souls from going there."

17. To return to the theme of the previous chapter, note here how the Lord's Prayer also implores God to "forgive us our sins." As Scott Hahn notes in his commentary, "Deliver us from evil" is a somewhat misleading translation. In the Greek of the New Testament, there is a definite article before the word *evil*. So Jesus actually commanded us to pray for deliverance from "*the* evil" or, more precisely, "the evil one." It makes a difference, and a rather large one at that. For there is only one evil, and that is sin. The only thing we really need to be delivered from is not trial, temptation, suffering, or the grave. The only real enemy is sin. See Scott Hahn, *Understanding "Our Father": Biblical Reflections on the Lord's Prayer* (Steubenville, OH: Emmaus Road, 2002), 65.

18. Tertullian, *On Prayer*, 1. See also *CCC*, no. 2761.

19. As St. Thomas Aquinas points out in his brief commentary: There are three things contained in this salutation. The first is due to the angel, namely, "Hail, full

of grace, the Lord is with thee, blessed art thou amongst women." Elizabeth, the mother of John the Baptist, contributes the second, namely, "blessed is the fruit of thy womb." The Church adds the third part, namely, "Mary," for the angel did not say Hail Mary, but only Hail, full of grace. And this name Mary, according to its meaning, fits the words of the angel, as will become evident. (Thomas Aquinas, "Saint Thomas Aquinas on the Hail Mary," *Catholic Dossier* [May–June 1996], http://www.ewtn.com/library/MARY/STTOMHMY.htm.)

CHAPTER 4

1. *Roman Catechism*, I, vi, 2 (*The Catechism of the Council of Trent*, trans. T. A. Buckley [London: Routledge, 1852], 61).

2. Augustine, *Enchirdion*, 97. *Enchiridion* is a word meaning "manual" or "handbook." Accordingly, this short catechetical work is sometimes also called in English the *Handbook on Faith, Hope, and Love*.

3. "We are to understand by 'all men,' the human race in all its varieties of rank and circumstances—kings, subjects; noble, plebeian, high, low, learned, and unlearned; the sound in body, the feeble, the clever, the dull, the foolish, the rich, the poor, and those of middling circumstances; males, females, infants, boys, youths; young, middle-aged, and old men; of every tongue, of every fashion, of all arts, of all professions, with all the innumerable differences of will and conscience, and whatever else there is that makes a distinction among men. For which of all these classes is there out of which God does not will that men should be saved in all nations through His only-begotten Son, our Lord, and therefore does save them; for the Omnipotent cannot will

in vain, whatsoever He may will?" (Augustine, *Enchirdion*, 103).

4. *Summa Theologiae*, Ia, 19, 6. Thomas's precise views on the subject are, in fact, quite complicated (e.g., God's "antecedently" willing that all will be saved is not, Thomas argues, incompatible with his actually willing that some be damned). A good discussion can be found in Joseph G. Trabbic, "Can Aquinas Hope 'That All Men Be Saved'?," *Heythrop Journal* 57, no. 2 (2016): 337–58.

5. William Thomas Walsh, *Our Lady of Fátima* (Garden City: Image Books, [1947] 1954), 220.

6. Hans Urs von Balthasar, *Dare We Hope that "All Men Be Saved"?*, trans. David Kipp and Lothar Krauth (San Francisco, CA: Ignatius Press, 1988).

7. Rob Bell, *Love Wins: At the Heart of Life's Big Questions* (New York: Collins, 2011).

8. Robert Barron, "Is Hell Crowded or Empty? A Catholic Perspective," March 30, 2011, http://www.wordonfire.org/resources/article/is-hell-crowded-or-empty-a-catholic-perspective/405/.

9. Scott Hahn, *The Lamb's Supper* (Doubleday: New York, 1999).

CHAPTER 5

1. Graham Greene, *The Power and the Glory* (New York: Penguin Books, 2015), 132.

2. St. Thérèse of Lisieux, *The Story of a Soul* (Charlotte, NC: St. Benedict Press, 2010), 88.

3. Ibid., 40.

4. Ibid., 6.

5. Fulton J. Sheen, *Treasure in Clay* (New York: Image Books, 2008), 127.

6. St. John Paul II, *Sister Maria Faustina: Biography for Canonization*, available at http://www.vatican.va/news _services/liturgy/saints/ns_lit_doc_20000430_faustina _en.html.

7. St. Faustina, *Diary*, no. 1588

8. See St. Faustina, *Diary*, nos. 1044–49.

CHAPTER 6

1. "Then, after the prayer is over you say 'Amen,' which means 'So be it,' thus ratifying with our 'Amen' what is contained in the prayer that God has taught us" (St. Cyril of Jerusalem).

2. For a good treatment of the significance of the "amen" in the Creed, see *CCC*, nos. 1061–65.

3. In fact, Jesus uses this phrase dozens of times in the Gospel of John and over thirty times in the Synoptics.

Select Bibliography

Apostoli, Fr. Andrew, CFR. *Fatima for Today*. San Francisco: Ignatius Press, 2010.

Cirricione, Msgr. Joseph A. *St. Joseph, Fatima and Fatherhood: Reflections on the Miracle of the Sun*. Charlotte, NC: Tan Books, 1989.

Gaitley, Fr. Michael E., MIC. *The Second Greatest Story Ever Told: Now Is the Time of Mercy*. Stockbridge, MA: Marian Press, 2015.

Johnston, Francis. *Fatima: The Great Sign*. Charlotte, NC: Tan Books, 1980.

de Los Santos, Sister Lucia. *Fatima in Lucia's Own Words*. Edited by Fr. Louis Kondor, SVD. 13th ed. Fátima, Portugal: Secretariado Dos Pastorinhos, 2007.

Martindale, Fr. Cyril, SJ. *The Meaning of Fatima*. London: Burns, Oates & Washbourne, 1950.

Ratzinger, Joseph Cardinal. *The Message of Fatima*. Rome: Confraternity of Christian Doctrine, 2000. http://www.vatican.va/roman_curia/congregations/cfaith/documents/rc_con_cfaith_doc_20000626_message-fatima_en.html.

Silva, M. Fernando. *The Shepherds of Fátima*. Boston: Pauline Books and Media, 2008.

Sheen, Ven. Archbishop Fulton J. "Our Lady of Fatima and Russia." In *Communism and the Conscience of the West*, 199–217. New York: The Bobbs-Merrill Company, 1948.

Walsh, William Thomas. *Our Lady of Fátima*. New York: Image Books, 1990.

Windeatt, Mary Fabyan. *The Children of Fatima*. Charlotte, NC: Tan Books, 2015.